Newport Pagnell
and the
Villages

Newport Pagnell has always played an important part in the life of this north-east corner of Buckinghamshire. For centuries it was a flourishing market town. It was a stopping place for travellers on the main routes between London and Leicester, Oxford and Cambridge. It was even considered to be of such strategic importance during the Civil War that it had a Parliamentary garrison.

In the first quarter of the 20th century, the town, as a trading and shopping centre, served a series of small villages whose residents either walked, drove wagons or took the new-fangled omnibuses to Newport to do their special shopping, to visit the fairs, to do their banking, see a Hollywood movie, or to catch a train to travel to work, to visit relatives — even to spend a day at the seaside.

But what were those villages like 50 and 100 years ago? We hope this book and its many pictures will give you some idea. We have been lucky to find people only too willing to talk about their home villages and loan us their old photographs and postcards. We have not set out to give a detailed history of each community, but to show you what places like North Crawley, Chicheley, Moulsoe and other villages looked like when they were so dependant on local employment and the "metropolis" of North Bucks — Newport Pagnell.

Astwood

ASTWOOD is the most north-easterly community within the old Newport Hundreds. In recent years, thanks to a bypass, it has returned to a more peaceful existence having suffered for years with main road traffic between Newport Pagnell and Bedford.

Like all North Bucks villages its prosperity was for centuries based on agriculture and the local manor. In the Domesday Book it is recorded as part of Hardmead parish, but gets its first ecclesiastical mention as Estwode (Eastwood) chapel when the Paganels owned the estate and gave the Church to the monastery at Tickford.

St Peter's Church, whose list of vicars dates from 1222, contains memorials to former owners of Astwood Bury including those from the Lowndes and Cranmer families. The porch of the church was demolished by a bomb during the 1939-45 war; the church roof was weakened and had to be propped up with a telegraph pole. Services were held in a lean-to built at the end of the church until the roof could be repaired with concrete beams replacing the old wooden ones.

An early picture of the Swan Inn, now called the Old Swan. It belonged to the Boswell Estate and was tenanted by John Wooding and then by his daughter Vi. The Wooding family, of Manor Farm, were by far the biggest employers in the village, hiring out three threshing machines — each unit containing a steam engine a threshing drum and an elevator. The family also employed carpenters, joiners, building workers and were the local undertakers.

The Church of St Peter's, Astwood, in the early 1900s

Astwood

This was the old main road. The thatched cottages to the right were demolished in the 1950s to be replaced by Council houses off the Cranfield Road. The corner of the Village Institute can he seen on the left. The white building in the centre was a shop but is now once more a private residence.

Another view of the Village Institute from the Cranfield Road junction. The pantiled building on the left, at the end of the Swan Inn, was a blacksmith's forge used once a week (Wednesday) by Walter Higgins of North Crawley. It has been demolished and replaced by a bus shelter.

This photograph was taken looking towards Bedford and shows Town Farm which belonged to Astwood Bury. All demolished to make way for executive homes.

These four cottages at Astwoodbury were part of Dovecote Farm and were last tenanted in the 1940s. Newport Pagnell Rural District Council condemned them as unfit for human habitation and ordered their demolition. The farmer refused to pull them down and they are still standing.

Bury Farm, now Astwood Grange

Broughton

Now a quiet backwater, Broughton was once a main road village with an infamous corner that claimed many traffic victims in the 1940s and 50s. Broughton has an historic church dedicated to St Lawrence with a list of Rectors dating back to the 13th century. On its walls are some of the finest frescos in the area.

Chicheley

Mentioned in the Domesday Book as Cicelai (Cicca's Clearing) this village straddles the main Bedford to Newport Pagnell road and in 1901 had 208 inhabitants. The oldest building is Grange Farmhouse, formerly Balney manor house, probably dating from the 15th century. The property belonged to the Mansel Family for many generations until sold to Sir Anthony Chester about 1620.

St Laurence's Church is of early English style and has effigies and brasses of early estate owners. The Classical style chancel was built by Sir John Chester in 1708, replacing the original ruined chancel.

Chicheley Hall (above), the great house built for Sir John Chester by Francis Smith of Warwick 1720-5, was bought by Earl Beatty after the Second World War and is now opened to the public during the summer months.

▲ *St Lawrence's Church with, on the left, the Vicarage, built in 1821 for the Rev S T Townsend. It housed War Agricultural Executive Committee workers in the 1940s.*

◄ *The war memorial with the Chester Arms pub and Home Farm in the background. The road between the two is Bedlam Lane, believed to be a corruption of Bethlehem Lane used by Tickford Abbey monks to reach their Grange Farm at Chicheley.*

▼ *Dedication in 1921 of the war memorial at the junction of the main road and the service road leading to the Vicarage, the Church and the rear entrance to Chicheley Hall.*

Chicheley

Mr Eric Litchfield with horse and cart outside the Chester Arms.

Thatched cottages in Bedlam Lane

Mick Litchfield's father cutting hay

Emberton

This is another village that has been saved from main road traffic by a by-pass — even though the new road meant the loss of one of its two pubs "The Bear". In the centre of the village is a clock tower, built in memory of his wife Margaret by the Rev Thomas Fry who was Rector at Emberton from 1804 to 1860. The tower became somewhat dilapidated in 1845 and a subscription was raised to have it restored.

A view of Emberton Clock Tower. Behind it is the much-altered home of Mr and Mrs Ellis and on the left in the foreground is the butcher's shop owned by the Lett family for many years

Another view of the Clock Tower at the junction of the main Olney Road and West Lane

Main Street with the village smithy on the left.

Emberton

▲*The village pump outside the home of the Robinson family which ran the village shop next to the Institute. These houses have now been demolished to provide an entrance to Forge Estate*

▼*Olney Road showing, on the left, the home of the Sams family so influential in village affairs in the last century.*

Filgrave

This village is always associated with its neighbour Tyringham. Indeed it did not rate a separate entry in the Domesday Book, being noted than as part of the Tyringham estate. Filgrave, though by now more heavily populated than its neighbour, even had its own church, dedicated to St Mary, the list of Rectors running from 1272 to 1547. The church eventually fell into disrepair and was demolished. Of its four bells, two were said to have been taken to Tyringham, one to Sherington and the fourth, which had rolled down Lower Ram's Close into the brook at the bottom of Cuckoo Pond, was afterwards dug out and taken to Emberton.

An early view of the Clock Tower donated by the Konig family to commemorate the Coronation of King George VI. It was designed by Sir Edwin Lutyens to blend with the 19th century cottages opposite.

North Filgrave Farmhouse which still has its Victorian postbox in the garden wall

The Cottages, built over 120 years ago and now much modernised. The small bricks used in their construction came from the village's own brickworks.

Filgrave

Children at the village school in the early 1920s

Hayrick-making on Mr Rossiter's Rectory Farm

Widening the Lane after the First World War. This kind of job was carried out by local men when there was not enough work on the village farms.

Gayhurst

Though one of the smallest villages in the district Gayhurst has an Elizabethan mansion, a Wren-style church, reputedly the biggest walnut tree in England and more than its fair share of history. An early owner of Gayhurst House, Sir Everard Digby, was implicated in the Gunpowder Plot and executed in London on January 30, 1606. He was said to have held meetings with other conspirators in secret rooms at the House and taken exercise, while being hunted, down passages that led to Digby's Walk and the River Ouse.

St Peter's Church

Another owner, Sir Walter Carlile, claimed to be the first Member of Parliament to drive to the House of Commons in a motor car.

During the 1939-45 war members of the Women's Royal Naval Service (WRNS), working closely with Bletchley Park, used top secret de-coding equipment at the House. It was later to become a public school and has now been turned into self-contained flats.

Nearby is the lovely little church of St Peter's, said to have been built in 1725 to plans by Sir Christopher Wren, the work being paid for by Mr George Wrighte, of Gayhurst House. Inside the Church is a monument by Roubiliac to Sir Nathan Wrighte, Lord Keeper of the Great Seal in 1721, and his son George.

The front of Gayhurst House, hardly changed from the time of the Gunpowder Plot

A view of the Church and House taken from the garden

Gayhurst

Cottages on the main Northampton Road, the route of which was altered so that the Squire could not see it from Gayhurst House!

Mill Farm Cottages ......

Mill Farm Cottages, on the banks of the River Ouse, up-stream from Gayhurst, with Mill Farm in the background. A German bomb dropped in the farm yard at 8pm on Saturday November 29, 1940. The six cottages were burnt down in 1943 and the stones taken by the Fermor Heskeths for use on their estate at Easton Neston.

...... and nearby Tathall End

The next village on the road from Gayhurst to Hanslope is the tiny community of Tathall End. It is famous for its brook (and its floods), for its former pub "The Greyhound" and for its association with the gamekeeper who shot and killed Squire Watts who was returning to Hanslope Park from church one Sunday morning in 1912

Hardmead

One of the smallest populated villages in North Bucks, Hardmead had 90 residents at the turn of the century. It has an interesting manorial history and an historic (though now redundant) church of St Mary which dates from the 12th century. There is a tradition that one of the church's bells is buried on the north side of the churchyard in the moat that once surrounded the Catesby family's ancient home, demolished some 250 years ago.

Great Linford

ONE of the villages swallowed by the new city of Milton Keynes, with new roles being found for the Church of St Andrew's, the lace-making school and alms-houses and the Manor, for so long the home of the Uthwatt family. The coming of the Grand Union two hundred years ago brought a new importance to this essentially agricultural village, providing a wharf to allow narrow boats to join the branch canal to Newport Pagnell. When that canal arm closed the route was used to take the new railway link between Newport Pagnell and Wolverton — and Linford became the first station.

Schoolchildren posing in the main street at the turn of the century. The Nag's Head pub can be seen on the left at the rear of the picture.

The thatched cottages in the same road pictured in the photograph on the previous page. The road wound its way over the canal to the Woolstones.

An early picture of St Andrew's Church.

The imposing Linford Manor, a picture taken by Harry Bartholomew, a Great Linford photographer, who did so much to record scenes of North Bucks before and after the First World War.

Lathbury

In the 1930s Lathbury was a typical tiny North Bucks village with an ancient church, its own parson, a big house, and groups of cottages attached to local farms. It had a well-used village hall, known as The Hut, and a small shop. Children walked to school at Newport Pagnell, only a mile or so away. Housewives trudged there to do their main shopping and Saturday night the farm workers made for the nearest pub, The Neptune, on the approaches to the North Bridges.

Nowadays the cottages, the barns and farm workshops have been turned into modern luxury homes. But the sense of community is still there as seen by the highly successful bi-annual event that turns Lathbury into one gigantic market for the day.

Mentioned in the Domesday book Lathbury has a well-documented history (it had its own grammar school in 1551) and its imposing mansion, rebuilt at the beginning of the 19th century, was bought from the Mansell family in 1904 by Col William Trevor who turned it into a military academy. His pupils became known as the Lathbury Gents.

Col and Mrs Trevor had as their butler Arthur Sheldon, with his wife as their cook/housekeeper. "Shelly" was a great sportsman. He captained the Newport Pagnell Cricket Club for many years and reached his own "century" after retiring to live in Tickford Street.

During the 1939-45 war Lathbury Park was requisitioned by the Army and Nissen huts were built in the grounds.

Council houses were built in the 1950s, Lathbury Park returned to residential use and Lathbury Inn, used for many years as a farm house, became a residential home for the elderly. The opening of this Inn, built to cater for the stage coach trade using the main London to Leicester route, co-incided with the coming of the railways, effectively killing road passenger traffic!

All Saints Church, now beautifully restored. It dates from Norman times and has interesting murals and memorials

Walter Sapwell (left) and
Harry Robinson shearing sheep
at Inn Farm in the 1930s.
The shearing machine was
petrol driven as electricity did
not reach the village until the
Army took over Lathbury Park
in the war.

A rustic scene in the 1930s.
The building behind the wall was
part of the cattle yard at
Inn Farm and was converted into
a house in 1979

Lathbury

Lathbury Park in its time a mansion, a military academy and a 1939-45 training centre for Army units

▶▼*Long-term Lathbury residents Mr Fred Sapwell and his mother with Max and Kristel Kretz with their son Martin. Max was a German prisoner-of-war who stayed behind to work for Turney Brothers at their Inn farm. His wife, Kristel, worked for several years at the Westbury Maternity Home at Newport Pagnell. All the buildings in the background belonged to Inn Farm and have since been demolished or turned into homes.*

▼*A van turning out of Church Road in the 1950s when the main Northampton Road was being widened. Home Farm, where the Adkins family lived, is on the right.*

Church Road, showing the elegant Rectory with its coach house. In the distance are three cottages, originally built as washhouses for the Lathbury coaching Inn on the main Northampton Road.

Little Linford

LINFORD Hall, the traditional home of the Knapp family for over 250 years, was demolished some forty years ago to make way for executive homes. The Knapps were formerly Lords of the Manor of Newport Pagnell and, as such, owned Bury Field Common. This small village also has an historic church, St Leonard's. Its two bells, housed in a small cote at the west end of the church, are believed to be among the oldest in the county. A former Rector, Moses Magoliouth (1877-1881), was one of the revisers of the Bible.

The derelict Linford Hall in the early 1950s

Milton Keynes

This is the village that gave its name to the new city, much to the chagrin of the then dominant town in North Bucks, Bletchley. Milton Keynes retains much of its rural charm despite the new development and has an active historical society. The modernised Swan Inn is a favourite eating place for city office workers. All Saints Church has been restored and the village school is now a community centre.

Almost hidden by the trees, All Saints Church, viewed from the road leading to Willen.

The Elizabethan style Rectory, built in the 17th century and refurbished in 1858.

Moulsoe

This village was in a real backwater until the building of Cranfield Aerodrome and the College of Aeronautics brought much traffic to its narrow winding roads. It still has many old buildings that can be found in the accompanying pictures.

In 1712 Moulsoe had 67 families and 270 inhabitants. There was still a population of 214 in 1891. One hundred years later, after the building of council estates and private houses, the figure was 236. The Church is dedicated to the Assumption of the Blessed Virgin Mary and its list of Rectors dates from 1233.

The last Rector, the Rev David Morgan-Evans, was appointed in 1938 and stayed until 1985 when he was the oldest Church of England incumbent in the country. He remained at the Rectory after retirement, until his death in 1992.

Tickford Park was the home of Mr Donald Fraser between the two wars. He had made his fortune from diamond mining in South Africa and was a keen horse breeder, keeping two stallions in stables next to the Carrington Arms, and brood mares in boxes in Water Tower field beside May Walk. Mr Fraser, who was crippled, followed the local hunt in a special half-track vehicle, a Citroen, similar to the first vehicles to cross the Sahara desert from north to south in the 1930s

Wisteria Cottage, on the left, built around 1580, was until the late 19th century the village alehouse called The Swan. During the 1880s licensee Joseph Hand also worked as a blacksmith and had a forge there. It was part of the Carrington Estate and when the Carrington Arms was built at the other end of the village it became a private house. Mr Donald Fraser, tenant of Tickford Park, bought the cottage in the 1920s and gave it to his cook/housekeeper Miss Eleanor Hewardine Thompson on her retirement. She can be seen standing by the gate. The next cottage is St Mary's and beyond that a group of three cottages which were pulled down in the 1960s in order to widen the road. In 1940 a Bren gun carrier failed to negotiate the sharp corner and made a large hole in the curved wall of Carpenter's cottage opposite.

Moulsoe

Tudor Cottage, Newport Road, a late 17th century building now much altered and known as Hillcrest.

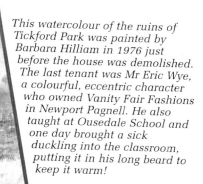

This watercolour of the ruins of Tickford Park was painted by Barbara Hilliam in 1976 just before the house was demolished. The last tenant was Mr Eric Wye, a colourful, eccentric character who owned Vanity Fair Fashions in Newport Pagnell. He also taught at Ousedale School and one day brought a sick duckling into the classroom, putting it in his long beard to keep it warm!

A pen and ink sketch of the 17th century Church Farm granary and byres which stood next to the Rectory. They were demolished in 1995 to make way for housing.

▲Mrs Gertrude George (1872-1943), formerly Mrs William Hilliam, standing at the gate of her cottage at the corner of Woodend Lane and Cranfield Road, now the site of Mr Albert Dorrill's bungalow. The cottage was demolished in 1960 after the death of Mrs George's daughter, Miss Ethelwynne Hilliam.

▼The christening party of Edmond Hilliam in the garden of Tudor Cottage in July 1969. Sitting under the pear tree from left to right, Mrs Kaye Pulsford, of Rose Cottage, the Rev David Morgan-Evans, Rector of Moulsoe, and Miss Margaret Salmons who also lived in the village. She was the daughter of Mr Lucas Salmons, co-owner of Salmons and Sons Coachworks (now Aston Martin Lagonda Ltd) and the Electra Cinema, Newport Pagnell

Moulsoe

The thatched
Methodist Chapel at Moulsoe
which was demolished by
volunteers and taken to the
Stacy Hill Museum at
Wolverton

Moulsoe Rectory, built in the
Queen Anne period on an earlier
moated site.

North Crawley

This parish is the third largest in the old Newport Hundreds and, thanks to local volunteers, has probably the best mapped and best used set of footpaths in the area. It had almost 1,000 inhabitants in 1851, but this figure dropped to 622 in 1891 as, like other North Bucks villages, it found young couples moving to the prosperous railway towns of Wolverton and New Bradwell. New development in the 1970s almost doubled the number of houses and bungalows in the village (population now around 750) and it has become a desirable "dormitory" for Milton Keynes and Cranfield, while still retaining its sense of community, its school, a shop and two pubs.

The approach to the centre of the village from Newport Pagnell. The second cottage on the right was a public house called "The Duke William" known locally as "The Jerry." It closed in 1906. District Nurse Monk lived in the cottage at the Folly Lane junction.

This view of the main street shows the three village pubs, the "Cock" and the "Chequers" on the right and the "Castle" (which closed in the 1960s) on the left. The houses jutting into the road, beyond the horse and cart, were demolished to make way for the Co-operative stores. Mrs Adderson, who was living at the Chequers at the time, was the first customer when the Co-op opened and was the last when the shop shut in 1997. The house on the right, behind the lady, was originally a group of Feoffee (charity) cottages. Between them and the "Chequers" is now the Village Institute built by Mrs Boswell around 1920. The house with the arch was where the ostlers from Crawley Grange lived and kept the wagons before the stables at Crawley Grange were built at the beginning of the last century. All footpaths were cobbled and the iron railings seen in the picture were taken down for the war effort in 1940.

North Crawley

The village church dedicated to St Firmin, a Bishop of Amiens in the third century. There are only two other churches with similar dedications in England. It has a finely decorated rood screen

The Rectory, now the home of Major J B Chester, was built in 1800 for the Rev R T Lowndes and occupied by the Selby-Lowndes family until 1899. It was previously the site of Handlo Manor. This picture was taken in the late 1920s.

High Street leading to Cranfield. The house on the left was built with bricks from the brickyard at Chicheley. On the right is the Congrgational Chapel now a private house.

A clearer view of the district nurse's house with the former Duke William pub which was a sweet shop before becoming a private house

The front on the Cock Inn facing the Waste Ground in the early 1900s. The man with the bike is William John Welch the licensee who was related to the Ruffhead family

Folly Lane, which provides a back road to Wharley End. The house on the left was formerly a butcher's shop run by Jordan Ruffhead whose other job was to empty the earth closets in and around the village. He was a well-remembered figure with his horse-drawn tank on wheels. He became very bent in later years (it was said through carrying the heavy sanitary buckets!) but he used to cycle into Newport Pagnell to fetch the Sunday papers and sell them standing on the Waste Ground. He was so bent that he recognised his customers by their shoes!

North Crawley

Crawley Grange said to have belonged to Cardinal Wolsey, confiscated by Henry VIII and later owned by the Hacket Family, then the Selby-Lowndes and later by Thomas David Boswell, younger brother of Johnson's biographer. The Grange has now been converted into flats. For years the village fete was held in the Grange gardens.

Chicheley Road showing the Council houses, some of the first to be built by Newport Pagnell RDC in the 1920s

In this group of North Crawley lace-makers the one on the right, Lizzie Wright, was the village postmistress.

Ravenstone

Five miles from Newport Pagnell is the village of Ravenstone which, despite its apparent isolation can lay claim to have had its own Priory and to have been the home of one of the most influential men in 17th century England, Chancellor Sir Heneage Finch, Keeper of the Great Seal and First Earl of Nottingham.

It was he who founded the 12 almshouses for six poor men and six poor women and orded that they should each be paid 3s 6d (17p) a week. His magnificent tomb is one of the features of All Saints Church.

There are still some lovely thatched cottages in the village, a tribute to the skill of local thatchers.

The district nurse with her bicycle outside her home that was always known as Nurse's Cottage. It still stands, though re-thatched and modernised. Mills Cottage can be seen in the distance

*These cottages in Abbey Way have been demolished and new houses built on the site.
The village pub, The Wheatsheaf, can be seen in the distance with Tommy Adams' bread cart from Stoke Goldington, nearby.*

*The cottage with the step is still standing, the smaller cottage being the home of the local thatcher.
The Wheatsheaf pub on the left is now a private house.*

Ravenstone

▲*These cottages on the left have been taken down and three houses built behind. The house on the right was formerly Robinson's farmhouse*

▼*The Post Office, now a private house called Mills Cottage*

▲*Mrs Richardson making lace outside the Post Office. Farther on, between the cottages, is the old Chapel, no longer standing.*

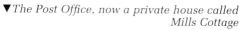

▼*Ravenstone Almshouses founded by Lord Chancellor Finch. Originally homes for 12 people they have been modernised and now provide six apartments*

This view of the village, near the turning to Stoke Goldington, has not altered much since the 1920s

All Saints Church, Ravenstone, contains the massive monument to Heneage Finch.

A print showing composite scenes of the Great Fire of Ravenstone. On Friday, September 24, 1897, sparks from a steam traction engine threshing corn from allotment holders, set fire to a thatched barn on Mr William Eyles' farm. A strong wind sent flames through the rickyard to an adjoining farm and several cottages. By the time the Newport Pagnell and Olney fire brigades had the blaze under control some ten buildings had been destroyed and 50 people made homeless.

Sherington

The Knoll at Sherington is, supposedly, the half-way mark between Oxford and Cambridge. In the 1920s there was a ceremonial burying on the spot of a hatchet by the rival universities. But this green area off the main Newport Pagnell to Olney road has also seen many local celebrations over the years from Coronation to Millennium festivities.

Sherington has grown considerably in recent years and has a fine community spirit. Villagers brought about the re-opening of its ancient pub The White Hart and set about the restoration of the parish church, the only one in England dedicated to the French bishop St Laud. Indeed, to raise money for the church, a group carried out a marathon cycle ride from the village's name sake Sherrington (with two rs) in Wiltshire.

Church End with St Laud's in the background. The large "Calgary House" on the left was one time in the ownership of Mr Tillyard whose brother Fred emigrated to Canada and founded a bakery business in Calgary. One of his descendants still lives in the house. On the right is the gable end of Sherington's fourth pub The Royal Oak which closed between the wars.

On the right can be seen the window of The Swan one of the village's two remaining pubs. Next door is a thatched cottage (originally two) the home of the Haynes family. When this picture was taken the Knoll was enclosed as it formed part of the garden to Pearcy Cottage. The fence was removed in the early 1940s. On the left is the Corner Stores and beyond the car The Crown and Castle pub which closed in the 1960s. Next door to that was Bill Clarke's blacksmith shop.

Looking towards Water Lane from the Knoll with West's general stores on the right hand corner. It is said that this house was orginally a pub the Rose and Crown in the 1700s and later became a butcher's shop. On the extreme right is an early reconstituted stone telephone kiosk just behind which can be seen the Jitty which was the only entrance to Hill's Yard where stood two-up-and-two-down cottage in which six families with over 30 children between them lived in the early 1900s

►Church Road in the 1930s. On the right is School Lane, formerly Parson's Lane as it led to the Rectory. The white-fronted house on the right was Wiliam Groom's blacksmith's shop with the forge nearest the camera. Gun Lane is on the left and the wall has long since vanished in the interests of road widening.

▼The Congregational Church built in 1822. The notable features are the staff cottages on either side, one tenanted by the cleaner and the other by the boilerman who kept the central heating sytem in working order. These cottages had to be built to support the main structure which was unstable on its own. The church was closed in the 1980s and is now five apartments.

Sherington

Looking up Park Road at the beginning of the last century. The village's own famous equestrian painter, Tom Ivester-Lloyd, lived in the tall house on the right with his son, Jack, who was an author. Note the interesting herring-bone stonework on the house on the left.

John Line's timber yard, taken in the 1920s with John and his two sons Bill and (at the front) Ben. The yard was in Church Road next door to the wheelwright's shop. The machinery was driven by a portable steam engine and provided all the timber for local needs.

This picture was taken in the early 1920s when the Oakley Hunt met on the Knoll. The footpath led to the village pump, unfortunately obscured by the grey horse. To the right can be seen C J Hind's wheelwright's shop now reconstructed at the Stacey Hill museum.

Another view of the same meet, showing the fence that enclosed part of the Knoll. The cottages behind were demolished in the 1930s

Stoke Goldington

In the early part of the last century Stoke Goldington was renowned as the home of the Whiting family whose steam traction engines travelled throughout the Midlands and East Anglia providing famers with ploughing and threshing services.

The main Newport Pagnell to Northampton road runs through the village which, apart from council and other small housing estates, has changed little over the years. It has a flourishing historical society which has photographed and listed all the buildings and has been a great help in the compilation of this booklet.

St Peter's Church, now isolated to the north-west after, it is believed, the centre of the village was moved following the decimation of the population by the plague.

Approaching Stoke Goldington from Northampton. This photograph, taken around 1900, shows the Rectory on the right. Following a fatal road accident in 1944 the Rectory wall and trees were demolished to make the corner less dangerous. The large building in the background was an off-licence run by the Bull family and had no connection with the White Hart pub next door.

This photograph was taken in the 1920s and shows the White Hart from the Newport Pagnell direction. It was orginally owned by the Newport Pagnell Brewery, but was later taken over by Charles Wells of Bedford.

On the left is Dag Lane taken about 1924 showing on the right Park Farm. Next door is the Hayward's Cottage demolished in the 1940s. Set back is the village hut, the centre of village social life at that time. It was owned by the Church but sold by the Rector in 1941 to some Jesuits from Cornwall. It fell into disrepair and was eventually demolished. Behind the hut can be seen the magnificent walnut tree said to be the largest in England which was also sold in 1941 by the Rector, the wood being used for rifle stocks. Adams the baker's delivery cart is just in front of Chestnut Farm.

Taken in the 1920s this picture shows the High Street looking towards Northampton. On the right is the Lamb Inn and next door is the oldest house in the village where Harry Armstrong lived. He was the main lace dealer in the district, trading in Olney where he founded the Bucks Lace Workers' Association. Next door is the Manse and beyond can be seen the two gables of the police cottages. On the left in the foreground is the cottage where lived Mr Cecil Darby, the village newsagent. Next door is Mrs Wesley's sweet shop with Mr Alfred Clarke the carrier's house beyond.

Stoke Goldington

The High Street looking south towards Newport Pagnell taken in the 1920s from under the branches of the chestnut tree planted to commemorate one of Queen Victoria's jubilees. Across the lane to the right can be seen Arthur Hill's tea rooms The big barn belonged to George Inn Farm. To the left, next door to Archway Cottage are the Reading Rooms built in 1882 and given to the village by J W Carlile. Unfortunately they were not endowed and the village sold them back to Sir Walter Carlile in 1922 for one shilling (5p). In 1980 his widow, Lady Elizabeth Carlile, gave the rooms back to the Parish Council. The end-on house with a first floor window is East Side Farm, home of the Whiting family. The Manse can be seen in the distance.

Looking back at the same area from the south Mr Hills' tea rooms are on the left. They did a brisk trade, particularly at weekends as they were listed in the Cycling Touring Club's Guide. There is a pavement the entire length of the High Street on the west side, but the east side has cobbles all the way down.

The end of the High Street looking up the Newport Road. The second house on the left was the home of Mr Tommy Adams, the village baker, where, on Sundays, people used to take their dinners along to be cooked. The war memorial stands on the village green, given to the village by Sir Walter Carlile in 1921. The White Lion then owned by Phipps later became the Hollow Tree restaurant. In the distance, on the left, can be seen the house which Mr Gibson, of Newport Pagnell, had built incorporating an elaborate Egyptian-style portico.

Tyringham

An isolated church, an elegant mansion overlooking the Great Ouse, a wonderful bridge and an impressive gateway leading from the main Newport Pagnell to Northampton road. These, with a few houses and farms, make Tyringham one of the most peaceful of villages

The mansion, built to plans by Sir John Soane in 1792, replaced an earlier building. In the early part of the last century it was the home of the Konig family whose members played an important part in the life of the district and carried out many alterations to the building. The Temple of Music was the scene of many a Sunday afternoon concert in aid of the local Blind Association.

The present Tyringham House, gateway and bridge were designed by Sir John Soane and are universally recognised as some of his finest work. They were built between 1792 and 1797 and are now Grade 1 listed. The photograph shows the gateway in about 1905. Note the post box and also the windows blocked up against vandalism, prevalent even in those days! Nicholas Pevsner in his "Buildings of England" calls the gateway "a monument of European importance".

The tower of St Peter's Church is the only original part of this 12th century building. The present church was completed in 1871 and designed by E J Tarver of the Arts and Crafts Movement. Inside there is a memorial dedicated to William Praed and his wife of Tyringham House. He was the first chairman of the Grand Junction Canal Company and there is a relief of a canal lock complete with narrowboat carved in the white marble. The Elizabethan House stood close by and in the churchyard there are early headstones dedicated to servants who worked in the House.

Tyringham

A similar view of the house showing the alterations and additions commissioned by Mr Konig in the early 1900s. The dome was designed by a German arhitect E von Ihne, who also gutted the Soane interiors. The forecourt with "sentry boxes" wrought iron gates, stone balustrading and formal fountain were designed by an English architect Charles Rees in 1914, as were the formal gardens around the house. Sir Edward Lutyens designed the two long pools, the Temple of Music and Bathing Pavilion in 1926.

The entrance hall, redesigned by von Ihne about 1920 showing the heavy German influence.

Mr and Mrs F A Konig in their walled garden with the head gardener's house in the background.

Tyringham

The stable entrance, looking through into the courtyard. The entrance to the harness room can be see in the distanced, round which is a fine stone portico which is the only piece to survive from the original house by the church

Tyringham Cottage, a misnomer for such a large house! Built in the Edwardian era it is now known as Park House and is a residential home for the elderly.

Weston Underwood

This village has a closer affinity to Olney and, of course, is famous for its association with that town's poet, William Cowper, who wrote about Weston Underwood's splendid views across the Ouse Valley and his own favourite Wilderness. Through the Throckmorton family the village was the centre of Roman Catholicism in the area. In more recent years it has become widely known through its zoo and flamingo gardens.

Easily recognisable, the village's main street, even 80 years after this picture was taken. On the left is Cowper's Lodge where the Olney poet came to live in 1786 - and where the church fete was held in 2000! The next large building is the Georgian "Stoneways" and beyond that the Cowper's Oak pub. Next comes the former forge run for many years by Charlie Covington. On the right is the village shop.

Another view of the street taken from the opposite direction showing the wall of The Wilderness. Hidden round the corner was the old village Reading Room and farther up the street on the right is the old ivy-covered Post Office.

The famous Knobs at the Olney entrance to the village. One of these imposing pillars was demolished in a traffic accident in the 1950s. When being replaced, the opportunity was taken to widen the road

The Avenue with Cowper's Alcove in the distance. Many of these trees were cut down in the 1930s

The old Roman Catholic Chapel, now a private house. Only one of the original windows remains.

Willen

FIFTY years ago one of the smallest villages in the area Willen had a London-style church, two farms and a series of farm cottages. Now, as part of the new city, it has given its name to a large housing area and a series of man-made flood prevention lakes that provide a haven for birds. Its dominant feature is still the church, now joined by the Peace Pagoda. One of its farms has been adapted to house the Hospice of Our Lady.

The two most important buildings eighty years ago, the church of St Mary Magdalene and, on the right, the village school

The Woolstones

It is difficult now to recall that these villages were once important communities on the main road between Newport Pagnell and Bletchley. One of the most famous residents of Little Woolstone was Mr William Smith whose steam plough invention, "The Woolstone System", revolutionised ploughing in Victorian and Edwardian eras. The much enlarged Barge and Cross Keys inns now have roles far removed from their original village pub days. The ancient Holy Trinity Church, Little Woolstone, is a good example of how a traditional building can be adapted to become a place of worship and a community centre.

The Church of Holy Trinity at Great Woolstone has, in recent years, been turned into a music centre and workshop for making and painting scenery for local theatre productions.

Newport Pagnell

No book about the villages would be complete without a series of pictures showing what Newport Pagnell itself was like 50 or more years ago. This photograph will bring back happy memories for those born in the 1920s and 1930s. These are some of the famous Bury Field Bushes, where nightingales sang, couples courted, familes went for walks and young Boy Scouts held campfires!

This was Bury Field before 1942, the year when the common was requisitioned, the great swathe of bushes and trees was uprooted and burned, and for probably the first time in its history the field was ploughed and sown with corn as part of Britain's bid to feed itself in war-time.

▲These ricks, built in the North Bucks style, were placed near the wall beyond which the present Queens Avenue houses were built. Building ricks was a specialised job. They contained enough sheaves for one day's threshing and sometimes the sheaves settled unevenly causing the ricks to tilt. If this happened long poles (known locally as Cranfield men) were used as stabilisers.

▼Carting sheaves in the Duffers (Dovehouse Close) on Bury Field. Mr Walter Sapwell is pitching sheaves to Mr Harry Robinson on the trailer. The driver of the second tractor is Fred Sapwell. In the background can be seen the Ash Hill water tower that supplied the town for so many years.

Newport Pagnell

▲*This building was erected in the early 1800s and became the Railway Tavern when the Newport Pagnell to Wolverton line was opened. The milepost on the left is still standing but gone are the gas lamps which drew their fuel from the gas and coke works in Caldecote Street, long since demolished and turned into a garage and car park. The Tavern remained a pub for years, being renamed the Newport Arms. Now it is an Italian Restaurant.*

▼*It is hard to realise that this creeper-covered building is the High Street house, still standing, that gave its name to Cedars Way.*

▲This view of the High Street shows the (then) new Post Office, gas lamps, the pillars of the Anchor Hotel, Odell's ironmonger's shop in the distance — and not a car in sight!

▼The cart-rutted, narrow St John Street. Most buildings on the left are still easily recognisable but on the right are homes, pubs and businesses that have passed into history — including Comptons the builders and undertakers, the Admiral Hood and The Marquis of Chandos pubs.

Newport Pagnell

This photograph of the ivy-covered Church of St Peter and St Paul was taken from Castle Meadow — known in those days as The Bully — with grazing cattle from one of the local farms, probably Woad Farm just across the river where the Lovat joins the Great Ouse.

The famous Iron Bridge showing the extra pinnacles on the Church tower and the chimneys of the terraced houses that lined Riverside.

▲Right on the outskirts of Newport Pagnell, at Wepener, is Caldecote Mill, once the home of world snooker champion Walter Donaldson.

▼The junction of the Ouse and Lovat Rivers taken from the cemetery

▲Cannon Corner before Sawbridge the butcher's shop was demolished to be replaced by the Midland Bank building. The Plough and the Anchor Hotel are on the left.

▼Tickford Street decorated for Queen Victoria's Jubilee

Standing bleak and isolated as one of the few buildings in Lakes Lane this former private house, now known as The Beeches, is a residential home for the elderly. On the right, near the gas lamp, is the kissing gate at the Jitty which leads to Bury Field.

Newport Pagnell

▲ *The Union, the Workhouse, the Spike, all names for the building that ended its days as Renny Lodge Hospital. Originally built in 1840 as a Poor Law Institution to house the poor and destitute, it also provided accommodation for tramps and "knights of the road" in return for a day's work breaking stones to keep local roads in repair.*

▼ *This was probably taken in 1911 when the bells at the Parish Church were recast. They were transported by rail to the foundry in Whitechapel.*

▲*A view of the flooded Ouse taken from the Church tower. Lawman's bakery and tea rooms can be seen bottom right with the Neptune public house at the North Square junction.*

▼*The viaduct, built over Wolverton Road near The Green to take the branch railway line from Newport Pagnell to Olney. The only remaining features of this ill-fated venture are the cuttings in Bury Field*

The Edwardian High Street with its wide pavements and multitude of shop blinds. In the far distance can be seen the stone pillars of the gates that led to the cattle market and Bury Field.

Still easily recognisable the High Street building that was in succession a school, the Town Hall, Church House and the Baptist Church. Now it has been turned into apartments.

Rogation-tide procession at the Parish Church, led by the Rev H Adeane Byard, the Vicar from 1933 to 1946

Newport Pagnell

Newport Pagnell had a lively
Chamber of Trade in the 1930s.
Here is a Shopping Week
parade led down St John Street
by a Scout band and
elephants!

A policeman on early morning
duty in a High Street decorated
for the 1937 Coronation

Odell's ironmonger's shop and the Parish Church in the early years of the century

Tickford Street floods in April 1908 with the old Kings Arms on the left

Two more views of Tickford Street.
Right, the George Inn on the right with Salmons motor works in the background.
Below, looking up to Highfield House on the Clay Lane (Chicheley Street) junction

A photograph taken in 1905 showing the famous Iron Bridge and the peaceful clear stretch of the River Lovat

An aerial view of Marsh End in the 1930s with the Caldecote Street-Silver Street junction at the bottom, the Bury Street Schools, the old Brewery buildings (top right) and the railway sidings (top left)

Newport Pagnell

Wolverton Road was widened in the 1950s.
Above, the improvements to the Linford Lane junction.
Below, workmen prepare to straighten out the dangerous Marsh Farm corner.

A new building goes up opposite Coales Mill which dominated the Caldecote Street, Broad Street and Station Road junction for so many years.

The narrow Church Passage which disappeared in the 1950s. The doorway leads to the bar of the Swan Tap, the haunt of ostlers and coachmen in the Coaching Era. In the distance can be see the two iron posts, still standing at the entrance to the Churchyard.

Newport Pagnell

Taken well over 100 years ago this photograph (exposed on a glass plate 10inches by 8inches) shows the kind of carriages made at Salmons and Sons Tickford Works. Now, of course, the site is the home of Aston Martin.

▲*Newport Pagnell postmen in 1908*

▼*Car body builders at Salmons and Sons' Tickford Street works, featured on a 1917 postcard*

Newport Pagnell

▲*St John Street demolition in 1957*

▼*Local historian and churchwarden, Mr Newman Cole, in the Tickford Street bakery that members of his family ran for 200 years.*

One of the biggest impacts on the life of Newport Pagnell in the last century came in 1959 with the building of the £16million stretch of the M1which skirts the town. Contractors John Laing had their headquarters off Wolverton Road and the photograph above shows initial work on the bridge spanning the town's link with Stony Stratford and Buckingham. Thousands of tons of earth were moved to make the embankments and the picture below is of giant Euclids at work in Little Linford Lane.

A helicopter taking off from the John Laing headquarters at Walnut Farm.
Below, the new motorway bridge begins to take shape

Acknowledgements

We are grateful to many people who have given so freely of their time in helping us compile this pictorial history of the villages. Without their enthusiasm and co-operation it would have been an almost impossible task.

Mr Brian Hunt kindly undertook to copy many of the original postcards and photographs. Our thanks go to him and to those whose pictures and memories we have been privileged to enjoy:

Mr and Mrs Gordon Adderson	Mr Edward Baylis
Mrs Hazel Brammer	Major J B Chester
Mr Barry Clayton	Mrs Betty Course
Mr F Doggett	Mrs Jo Duncombe
Mr Derek George	Mrs Marion Hansford
Mrs Barbara Hilliam	Mrs Dorothy Martin
Mrs Peggy Parsons	Mr Alan Richardson
Mr Fred Sapwell	Mr Philip Smith
Mrs Vera Smith	Mr Ron Unwin
Mrs Jill Whiting	Mr and Mrs Denis Adams

We are particularly grateful for the help received from members of the Newport Pagnell Historical Society and the Wolverton and District Archaeological Society.

Sarah MacLennan

Gerald Stratton

Newport Pagnell, November 2000

Other Historical Society publications include:

They called it Newputt
by
Peter Adams

The Bucks Standard
by
Gerald Stratton

Newport Pagnell in the Nineteen Fifties
by
Gerald Stratton

One More for the Road
by
Don Hurst & Dennis Mynard

St John Street - From the Cradle to the Grave
by
Don Hurst

Available from Newport Pagnell Historical Society (telephone 01908 611683) and selected bookshops.